Bless you as you read this book.
Liz Agboaye

Agboaye

When Things GO WRONG

Words can motivate & encourage

STEP OUT CREATIVES PUBLICATION

WHEN THINGS GO WRONG
Isi Agboaye

Birmingham, UK
ISBN 10: 0-9553819-0-8
ISBN 13: 978-0-9553819-0-4

First Edition

Pictures by Ron Sutton
Cover Design by Andy Goulsbra

For copies of this book,
STEP OUT Workshop & Seminar booking:
Phone: 07960 118265
Email: stepoutmails@aol.com
www.stepoutcreatives.com

Printed in Great Britain by Askew Printers,
Doncaster, DN4 5HZ, www.askewprinters.co.uk

DEDICATION

To my dear mother,
Ejemen;
Iyiose & Oseta

APPRECIATION

I am thankful to God, friends and family;
for encouragement, thankful for
all the prayers, support,
proofreading, etc.
Thanks.

INTRODUCTION

Things will certainly go wrong. It may be a pin prick, loss of earning power, fire in an estate, stress, illness, death in the family or an offence by anybody. At such periods in our lives, we need appropriate words – more than anything else to soothe our hearts and troubled souls.

Meaningful words prepare us to handle issues that life throws at us, so, we would be able to tackle obstacles that assail us; knowing that we can overcome them and advance further. This is how a mature character is built, allowing one to see life in a better perspective with glowing testimonies.

In times of despair and frustration, a word aptly applied, as shown in this book, will go a long way to heal wounds and mend broken hearts. Such words are lifelines to a sinking soul. These lifelines are similar to the words of our saviour Jesus which are spirit and life – meeting great needs.

USES OF THIS BOOK

- You may read this book to acquire coping skills and wisdom in times of need. It may also be part of a resource guide for the resolution of inner conflicts.

- This book may also be read as part of a daily devotion with friends and family; looking closely at the ideas expressed relative to Bible verses.

- This book is anticipated to be a valuable tool for evangelism and discipleship. It may also be valuable as a daily companion in any setting like a lonely prison cell, hospital, etc.

- It could be a useful tool for group discussions in conferences related to deep psychological needs that may be prevalent within Christian circles.

ABOUT THE AUTHOR

Born in Calabar, before the Nigerian-Biafran war, the early years of my life were marked by a terrible illness. I was told by my parents and siblings that I survived miraculously because some faithful people prayed. Maybe that is why I am always looking for avenues to give something back to others as a form of gratitude to God.

As a pastor, missionary worker with PFM, dramatist, and classroom teacher, my daily experiences also inform my style of writing; enabling me to motivate and empower as many as possible.
I love positive words - known in my part of Africa as 'sweet' and valuable; and I enjoy creating with words towards exploring the issues that affect us all so deeply.

As a motivational speaker, I draw freely from daily human experiences. I see mankind as one, or unified in laughter and tears – with buckets of needs – all concealed in smiles. I strongly believe that there is power in positive words –

especially when connected to the living word of God.

I studied Drama at University of Jos and University of Ibadan respectively; and Adult Education at University of Wolverhampton. I am blessed with a wife and children who have gifts and talents that keep inspiring me. Furthermore, I am eternally thankful to my brothers, sisters and brethren for all their love, motivation and great support.

The LORD [is] my rock, and my fortress, and my deliverer; my God, my strength, in whom I will trust; my buckler, and the horn of my salvation, [and] my high tower.
Psalms 18:2 - KJV

WHEN THINGS GO WRONG

1.

GOD, A SOLID ROCK

1.
There is always that voice that seems to tell you that all doors are closed. Reject it. God will make a way in your situation. Do not be tempted to shut the door of your heart. How will God gain access and help you in time of need?

2.
Ask God to take control of everything and guide you at this time like no one would. Do not take your eyes off the Lord for a second; see Him in your mind's eyes looking out for you.

3.
When things go wrong, God should not be the last to know. This is not the time to phone a friend or relative. Put God first and talk through the issues with Him. Ask God to lead you to someone equipped

with keen ears to listen and pray through it all with you. Most counselors may have good intentions and knowledge but God has all the clues.

4.
You may be hard pressed; things may have really gone wrong. Do not think that you know it all. Ask the Holy Spirit to help and guide you through. You certainly need supernatural help.

5.
Remember that you neither created yourself or the world around you. God created you, and knows the number of hair on your head and knows what is best for you.

6.
Do not seek answers from many sources; especially from carnal self-willed people. You may get many vague answers, short cuts and choices that lead to nowhere. Trust God and the simple instinct He has given to you.

7.
The situation you have found yourself may be an opportunity for you to change your tactics or your style of doing things. Associate every aspect of recent events or happenings with the word of God. Sleep over your decisions and don't utter negative words, or take hasty steps.

8.
Take time to meditate on the Psalms and draw strength from God. Read the book of Proverbs and gain wisdom and common sense from God. He will renew your strength through His word.

9.
When you have waited for awhile and there is no breakthrough, do not ask God to take the back seat, in order to solve your problems yourself.

10.
This is the best time to trust God and rely on Him with all humility; trusting Him with all your heart, soul and being - even in the darkest hours of your life.

11.
When things go wrong, take time to press on. It may not be the end of the road for you. It may be an opportunity for you to prepare for greater things ahead.

12.
Remember that you may be frail and weak; but God is all powerful and strong. Ask Him to give you strength, and the special grace to carry on.

13.
You can never force or push things. Solutions do not just occur the way we wish them to; but with perseverance and faith, God will put things in place for you.

14.
You may not be able to see the future at this time, but God sees it all and knows the beginning and the end of the situation you are facing. It pays to listen to Him and hold tightly to His hands.

15.
Do not speak negative words; and the Bible encourages us to put a hold on our

tongues. Don't forget that words can create or paint bleak outcomes within and around us.

16.
You must come to that point where you believe that, even if the whole world should collapse around you, God is able to reverse the situation.

17.
Don't be quick to accuse others; see God at work in every situation and refuse to give credit to the devil. Moreover, quit seeing the devil in all things; just let your mind be saturated with God.

18.
Smile. Let your smile progress into laughter; keep laughing and key into the spiritual; meet with God at His throne and have fun with your living God and the angels. Smile.

19.
Rejoice, sing and dance with God your father. If you have never discovered that you can dance with God, this is the time to dance with Him. See yourself in

the spirit dancing before His throne and giving Him praise, and more praise.

20.
Be thankful to God. If the word of God says that we should give thanks in all things, that's exactly what we should do.

21.
With God, opportunity knocks more than once. Keep looking up; don't give up. In God there are always open doors. Keep on knocking with your prayers.

22.
This is a time to find the true will of God for you. Do not wait for anybody to tell you that; let God speak to your heart, and open your heart and ears to receive His word.

23.
Humbly come to Christ with all your burdens: stinking rags, failures, stress, fears and disappointments; He will give you that desired rest.

24.
Know that God is interested in a tiny sparrow and He will certainly be greatly interested in you. We often see our problems, but fail to see God standing by to lead us through. Why should you magnify your problems and see less of God's power?

25.
Although human touch is imperative, look beyond it; ask God to touch you with His supernatural hands. When you meet with Him, you would not depend on mere physical touch.

26.
Count your blessings. Think of all the great things God had done in the past for you. Believe that the present needs are not beyond Him, and He will still meet you at the point of your need.

27.
Do not think that you are trapped and finished. God opened the prison door for Peter, and saved Daniel from the jaws of hungry lions. He will free you from your problems.

28.
This is a time to stay calm and focused. Stay absolutely calm in mind, body and spirit. Create a calm environment all around you with comforting words.

29.
Do not compare yourself to anybody or think about any terrible thing that may have happened to someone you know. Trust God to take you though the situation.

30.
Be honest with yourself. Realise where you have gone wrong and you may begin to fix things right from that point.

Behold the fowls of the air: for they sow not, neither do they reap, nor gather into barns; yet your heavenly Father feedeth them. Are ye not much better than they?
Matthew 6:26 - KJV

2.
JUST BELIEVE

31.
If you find yourself in trouble or a difficult situation, you will certainly crawl out of it - especially with God's help.

32.
Accept the peace of God; dwell in it and let it flood your heart through and through.

33.
Reflect on the idea that you came naked into this world, and naked shall you depart. Nothing in the whole world is a big deal. Let that make a strong impact on your character as you prepare to totally submit yourself to God and accept His will.

34.
Learn to face that situation with boldness and do not run away and hide.

35.
Let the light and the power of Christ illuminate your heart. Stand by His powerful light and let it consume all the darkness around you.

36.
Let self-motivation spring from within. Do not expect others to do it for you. Motivate yourself.

37.
Be inspired by every little thing around you; ask God to teach your hands to create wealth.

38.
It is perfectly all right to shed tears; but remember that in order to progress, it may be necessary to begin to dry your tears and ask God to take control.

39.
Ask God to forgive your faults. Do not condemn yourself and place yourself in a worse state than your initial condition.

40.
If you created the mess, you can also clean it. Be honest - ask God to help you sort things out.

41.
Once again, think twice before you take any step. Hasty decisions seldom lead to positive ends, or produce helpful results.

42.
You are not perfect. Walk towards God's light, wisdom and perfection. He alone is perfect.

43.
Pride stagnates - keeping you glued to one spot. It neither brings progress nor prospers one; but continuously gives you a false image of yourself.

44.
Choose to be encouraged. God lifted Joseph from that pit of humiliation; He saved Daniel from the den of Lions; He can lift you from any pit that you may find yourself in – God will lift you up.

45.
Think about your possessions in Christ and in heaven. What will it really profit you to gain the whole world and lose your soul?

46.
Ask God to forgive any known or unknown sins. How long would you dwell in unwholesomeness and sin?

47.
Quit struggling. Submit that heavy load on your mind at the cross and replace it all with the joy of the Lord Jesus which is your strength.

48.
It's time for you to realise that faith is the key to reaching great heights, to reaching all known success in life, to climbing all mountains, and securing a place in heaven.

49.
Cling on to every word of God that promises you life and favour, calling things that do not exist into existence.

50.
Believe that you can glow again – that you can shine out and reach your greatest potentials.

51.
You are not alone. Trust God to see you though it all; and do not forget, even this too will pass away.

52.
Remember that pain is inevitable in life. Thank God for your situation and keep holding on to God – He will bring the relief you seek.

53.
You need a dose of perseverance. 'Difficult' you may say, but still, all you need is a dose of more perseverance.

54.
Be patient. Learn more patience as you travel on; the journey will soon be over.

55.
When did you last take some time to rest? When last did you last lie under the

sun, roll on the sand like a child, or enjoy yourself swimming?

56.
Investigate or research that problem. Find out all about it and how you can overcome it. God is not against knowledge; ask God to open your eyes.

57.
Ask God to lead you to someone who may be able to assist you. Be honest and give that person the true picture of what you are going through.

58.
Take time to be yourself. You are unique, and God is interested in you.
Be yourself and appreciate all the good gifts within you. Do not think that you have to be like others before you can 'fly'.

59.
It may be necessary to sort out your thinking and abandon the negative images that keep you tied to failure.

60.
Think about the Hebrew names of God and meditate on the particular name that relates to your needs.

61.
Think through the situation – it makes sense to think – just think it through. A pen and paper may help you sort out your ideas, as you write them out. God works through our imagination to correct problems around us.

62.
Sort out your finances; put alternative ideas and options in motion. Maybe you should think of creating more wealth through your talents rather than borrowing more money.

63.
This is the time when you could be most vulnerable; take care and be very observant so that no one takes advantage of you.

64.
Whereas there may be wisdom in the words you hear around you, a

multitude of counsel, keep your ears open to that still small voice of God.

65.
If you are feeling sorry for yourself all day long, self-pity will flood and overtake your mind. All that will be reflected back to you will be self pity and nothing but self pity.

66.
You may be invited to the camp of those who put themselves down. If you find one reason to put yourself down, others will find more reasons to put you down.

67.
Do not embrace defeat, or accept that you have always been destined for failure. Refuse to accept the negative position that some folks have consigned you.

68.
If you grumble, you may crumble under that heavy weight. Praise and worship God in your heart.

69.
Fix up; dress up, walk straight and prepare to conquer the world again. Let a stream of self-confidence flow through you–taking root in you.

70.
There will still be some tossing and turning and tears of frustration that may flow from your eyes; it is inevitable – but do not stay in this frame of mind.

71.
God's eyes are ever turned to the direction of His children – but are your eyes turned towards God?

72.
Support others. Think about how to create peace and happiness for others. Selfishness does not encourage creativity. As you create for others, you will indirectly create the best for yourself.

73.
You may be homeless, but you are certainly not hopeless. Be comforted and not disappointed.

74.
Recent negative events may be a ploy to distract you from your goal or an important task that may yield a load of blessings.

75.
If you did something wrong, just admit that you did it. Don't say that the devil made you do it. You may be waiting for too long admitting your fault, and moreover you may be inviting the devil to help you commit a worse crime.

76.
Change your speech or confession. Be positive. Mind your language and say only what Christ would say and do only what Christ would do.

77.
Do not abandon the ship or the team; you may need them soon. You may be the one to save them, or they may be the ones to save you.

78.
If you prayerfully listen, God would speak to your heart.

79.
Prepare to forgive others, giving them a second chance. God will love you more for doing just that, since Christ gave us a second chance when he died on the cross for us.

80.
See God leading you to his green pastures; although you are in the midst of drought or deprivation in your life.

81.
See God restoring your soul. It may seem impossible, but he has the power and he is restoring your soul, bringing calm, comfort and peace like a river.

82.
See God leading you through this valley of the shadow of death. Do not wait to see a spectacular miracle before you believe that He is capable of taking you through any danger.

83.
See God shielding you through that dark path. God will see you through.

84.
See God's rod and staff comforting you – see Him sending His array of angels to minister to you.

85.
See God preparing a table of great bounties before you, right in the presence of your enemies. Moreover, God anoints your head with oil.

86.
See your cup running over; and see goodness and all mercy following you down the streets and through the highways, and you are still dwelling in the house of the Lord forever and ever.

87.
Remember that the whole treasures in the whole world belong to God. Do not think for a second that they belong to man. Walk tall – be confident – your father, God, owns the world and all those in great and small positions.

88.
See your disappointment as a divine intervention. It may just be an opportunity for a breakthrough.

89.
Whatever happens, you will not lose the battle because God is on your side. Wherever things turn to, God will take sides with you even till the very end of life.

90.
Realise that you have a heritage in Christ. That heritage is solid, sure and confirmed in heaven.

91.
Consider the situation of the woman with the issue of blood. Her pathetic story in the New Testament should encourage us all. If she was not bold, she would have missed her blessings, and would not have got another opportunity again. Touch the Lord Jesus where you are and receive your blessings by faith.

92.
The battle of life is not between you and the devil; it is between God and the devil. Your part is to trust God to protect and cover you at all times. Moreover, God has won the battle through the saving power of the blood of Jesus.

For my thoughts *are* not your thoughts, neither *are* your ways my ways, saith the LORD. For *as* the heavens are higher than the earth, so are my ways higher than your ways, and my thoughts than your thoughts. **Isaiah 55:8-9**

3.
BE FOCUSED

93.
You may be tempted to take your eyes off the cross; do not. Keep your eyes focused on the cross.

94.
Magnify God in your heart; do not magnify your faults – not for one second. Give them all to Jesus and run your race with confidence.

95.
Appreciate drops of mercies – they may not be much – but just appreciate where God is taking you.

96.
It may be necessary to relocate your abode or shift your base after proper consultation with the Holy Spirit. That may spur some motivation and inspiration.

97.
Avoid an unhealthy competitive spirit and unending rivalry – which breeds strife and more stress.

98.
Motivate yourself even when nobody thinks about you. Do to yourself the same good that you wish for others.

99.
It may not be easy to take a step of faith; but you still have to take it in order to win.

100.
Seek to receive God's revelation about the problem you may be facing. Ask God to tell you what he thinks about the problem.

101.
There may be many suggestions but not one solution; there may be many doors, but none may be your entrance or exit point.

102.
A jam or clogged situation may be an opportunity for God to teach you new things, and point you in a better direction.

103.
This may be the time to wait upon the Lord Jesus and renew your strength.

104.
You need to hold on to hope and see the greater picture.

105.
Take consolation in the fact that there are eyes that see all and hands that are waiting to lift all burdens. They are the eyes and hands of God.

106.
Also take consolation from the fact that God hears your cry; He knows the beginning, the middle and the end. God knows how you feel.

107.
It makes sense to trust in God; He knows how you were formed in your mother's womb – and He knows the end.

108.
Dwell in God's word; read the Bible.

109.
Say this to yourself:
Before my frame
Learnt to roll
Before my frame
Learnt to crawl
Before my feet stretched to walk
Before I ran with feeble legs,
God knew me then; and still knows me now.

110.
Tell yourself that:
God created you for a purpose;
God's purpose in your life is positive and will come to fruition.

111.
Know that, at every turn of the way, there will be opposition; there will be wars; there will be distractions. Believe

God; there is life and light at the end your dark tunnel.

112.
Remember others who are going through the same situation you have found yourself in – pray for them.

113.
Do not be seen in places and with people that would not glorify God. It is the will of God that you remain with God's people at all times – not forsaking the assembly of the brethren so that you would gain strength.

114.
Watch and pray; wait for God's will and purpose even if nothing seems to be happening at first.

115.
Money is not the main source of power. There are other things that we should ask God to give us; and most important among these is wisdom, more wisdom and extra wisdom for the journey.

116.
Be thankful – let your song of thankfulness ring out loud from a pure heart. Burst into singing and joyful songs filled with words of thankfulness.

117.
Don't worry. Do not let the pain of the current stress or problem stick to your mind, and rob you of life and joy.

118.
Prepare to activate God's Angels to carry out the plans of God for your sake. You will not be able to carry out certain tasks on your own – let Angels storm out on your behalf.

119.
Make a positive happy plan for yourself. Not a negative sad plan. Plan to be happy.

120.
Don't plan revenge; there is no need to pay back evil for evil even when it would make you to feel better, and when many expect you to do so.

121.
Know this one fact: a tree cannot grow to a great height in one day. Do not expect a miracle instantly; rather, seek to know the giver of miracles – God.

122.
See the fact that nothing is permanent. What is hot today would be cold tomorrow; and what is rough today, may be smooth or calm tomorrow.

123.
It may be difficult at first; but keep holding on – keep holding on, and riding out the storm with God's help.

124.
God mends broken hearts; and the Bible makes us see that there's peace and soothing cure in God.

125.
Do not be too proud to ask for help; do not fail to ask many questions – though you are not obliged to act on them all.

126.
Ask more than one person for the right direction; knowing that in a many suggestions, you would know the better way. However, do not fail to confirm with God so that you do not get confused.

127.
Do not neglect the counsel of old folks and more experienced people. Some may seem senile, but their words may be golden. Moreover, they have been there, done it and have the badge of experience.

128.
Learn to forgive; meaning that you have let go of that debt and forgotten it; that you would not think or speak about it anymore.

129.
Do not allow yourself to be sunk in a well of guilt. That has always been the plan of the evil one - to erase your confidence and project a picture of guilt. Christ has set you free by his blood.

130.
You are permitted to be angry, but do not sin with your mouth, your heart and your attitude.

131.
Choose your words carefully; people are different, and they react to words differently.

132.
Do not put others down. Do all you can to motivate, cheer, and build their self - confidence.

133.
Keep the team spirit; work as one and have the same focus within the fellowship of believers and body of Christ.

134.
Do not let your temper rule you out of God's positive book. Know the antics of the enemy as an accuser and destroyer. You do not have to win an argument to excel in life.

135.
Do not expect everybody to help you, or to see things from your point of view - put your trust in God.

136.
Maintain your sense of humour.
Your ability to laugh and make others laugh may be the greatest weapon that you have at this time.

137.
Nothing is as sweet as maintaining a sweet attitude, and a sweet spirit – an attitude that is cultivated from within.

138.
God may not intervene instantly. Even if He does not intervene, keep holding on to His word.

139.
Stand firm and see the salvation of the Lord. The problems and foes you see today, will not be there very soon.
They rage
The curse
They tear apart
They tempt.

Stand firm and see the salvation of the
Lord. The enemies you see today,
you will not set eyes on them soon.

They infuriate
They intimidate
They victimise
They crucify.
Stand firm and see the salvation of the
Lord. The issues you see today,
you will not set eyes on them soon.

140.
Strongly believe that God knows you
deeply.
God cares
God cares
He is willing to lend a hand at all times;
And He cares.

141.
Never fail to see that true motivation
comes from God.
He knows all you can accomplish
He knows your ability
He reads your thoughts.

He promotes
He elevates

He appreciates you
He will make you shine.

He knows all you can accomplish
He knows your ability
He reads your thoughts

He appreciates you
He will decorate you
He will lift you up
He will make you laugh.

142.
Thank God for the gift of life – remember, when there is life, there is hope.
Even when all things fail,
God will still be God –
and He will always be there for you.

143.
Make up your mind to walk on the water; go for it! Keep moving, even when you falter after a few steps; do not look back – keep on moving. Peter would have thanked you if you told him this a day earlier before the sinking incident.

144.
Believe deeply within you and be convinced that you can do all things through Christ who gives you strength.

145.
See and think the best of all folks.

146.
Never underestimate the power of the one who knows that you may sink when you have little faith. Jesus is always watching out for you.

147.
Remember the story of the great man of God from Bristol. He had orphans in his care and there was no bread or a drop of milk; he had sad hungry children to feed. He asked them to pray and suddenly there was a knock on the door. Soon there was bread. Soon again, another knock on the door, and there was milk. His name is George Muller; the rest is now history – but he was human – just like you. God can still provide all our needs.

148.
This is a good time to look back at the miracles of Christ; the great power of God displayed in Elijah and Joseph, the power of God shown through Moses and the people of Israel in the wilderness.

149.
Know that wisdom is not always closely linked or tied to book knowledge.

150.
Realise that you are only human. You may still toss and toil in gloom, or wonder why help is far away. If you let go of the hands of Jesus, you will be lost in the crowd.

151.
Make sure that you are not dwelling in ignorance and living outside the true word and will of God.

152.
Ask God to teach you new things that will increase you greatly in many ways.

153.
Remember that God put Oases and streams in the most unusual places; the desert. Ask God to put his best resources in unusual places for you.

154.
No matter how long you stay in that horrible condition you find yourself in now, if you believe that you are coming out, you will certainly come out of it and no power on earth can keep you down.

155.
Do not think for one second that you are no longer a child of God. God loves you the way you are – although it is not an excuse to die in sin.

One [thing] have I desired of the LORD, that will I seek after; that I may dwell in the house of the LORD all the days of my life, to behold the beauty of the LORD, and to enquire in his temple.
Psalms 27:4

4.

IGNORE FLAMING TONGUES; MOVE ON

156.
Do not entertain the belief that all Christians would rush to assist you when things go wrong; or even that those who even show up would be of any assistance.

157.
Do not run to the world for help, thinking that because you have been offended by a few Christians, non-believers are you best alternative. The scriptures warn us not to love the world.

158.
Keep the door of your heart open to any idea that the Holy Spirit may drop in at this particular time. Write down the vision that comes to you. You may be the Joseph that will lead many to deliverance.

159.
Be strong in the Lord; put on the whole amour of God. This means that you should say it, visualise it and walk in it daily.

160.
Ask the Holy Spirit to teach you how to pray deeply.

161.
Take responsibility for your actions and ask God to lead you through.
Tell God that you are ready,
Ready to be brought out of the pit,
Out of the terrible pit
Out of a terrible mud
He is setting your feet on the rock and establishing your steps.
You are soaring
Like the ready Eagle - gliding with grace.

162.
Ask to be helped. Mind readers are rare theses days - just say what your needs are – say something.

163.
Do not see the Church service as boring; expecting your problems to be solved instantly. It pays to wait, wait upon God and seek to receive in the most appropriate time.

164.
God may speak to you through any source; He even used a Donkey to speak to someone in the Bible - Balaam.

165.
It is not impossible for God to lead you through a period of lack to a phase of abundance.

166.
Forgive yourself; even if everyone else refuses to forgive you. Accept that God has forgiven you; act as though you have been forgiven.

167.
Be thankful to God and those who came to your rescue. Show them great appreciation. Learn to say 'thanks'.

168.
God may be teaching you to swallow a pill of humility or modesty – do it with all joy.

169.
The Lord may also be teaching you to learn to stay for a long time in His presence in prayer, praise, fasting and supplication.

170.
Appreciate those who point your faults out to you. They truly love you and are keen to save your soul.

171.
Rethink your habits and attitude; begin to put things right.

172.
You can walk straight into God's CLINIC; there are no opening and closing hours; no fees, no receptionists – no forms to fill – none.

173.
Not even death can separate you from the love of God; No tomb – no grave

can stop you from His love and peace at the end.

174.
Reactivate yourself and your environment; begin to love yourself and put your environment right.

175.
Ask yourself sincere questions about how you have treated yourself and others, and effect a change.

176.
Prepare to reclaim more than you have lost; take stock of all that the devil has stolen from you and prepare to claim it back.

177.
The biological clock only exists in our minds, but not in the mind of God who makes all things new.

178.
Learn to say 'sorry' - it costs nothing. Moreover, it comes in one simple word. Just say it and move on.

179.
Getting out of your problem does not depend on who you know or what you know – but on God.

180.
The track of true friendship can still be retraced and the benefits utilised in this situation.

181.
Do all you can to be assertive in the presence of the devil; do not be passive.

182.
Learn to take your turn; God will never forget you even though He seems to reward those around you first.

183.
It is not what people say that matters; it's what God says that counts at the end of the day. So where will you tune your ears and mind to?

184.
Tell yourself that:
You will never complain,
cry, scream, or seek for attention.

185.
Hold on to God, even if all the clocks in the world stop ticking; believe that God will take you to your destination in his own special time.

186.
Your vision may be blurred; images may be dim with nothing in sight. Voices may become a great cacophony of noise – meaningless babbles – and patience may not come in many words – but one word will do; wait.

187.
Just say:
I will not blame God for my situation.
I know that my God moves in mysterious ways.

The hands of God are valiant
God will make a way for me
I have no stubborn will
I do not hold on to vain opinion
I lay my heart bare before God
I am sincere in this matter
I will not blame God for my situation.

188.
Seek to work against your number one enemy; the devil. He sneaks into plans, ideas, and tracks. He comes to kill to steal and to destroy; shutting open doors and opening shut doors.

189.
You will notice that the more you blame others, the more you will make your case weak, and you would soon shift from your power source.

190.
See your situation as a learning curve; a school lesson; and advancement to greater heights. The lessons may be hard, but the graduation will be sweet.

191.
You may have the impression that great achievers never had problems in the past. They certainly did and still do have problems.

192.
Prepare to be used by God to teach or encourage others through your great

experience. Many would be greatly blessed.

193.
God may be about to turn your mountain into a plain; he may soon part the red sea before you and lead you through dry land.
He may just be making all the crooked paths ahead of you straight; and making the impossible possible, and stretching your rich plains farther than the eyes can see.

194.
Do not be a slave to technology, thinking that man's invention will see you though. Mankind has limits; and where man stops, God continues with great miracles. Moreover, God created the source of all things; and knows all things.

195.
Do not fail to give; you may be opening closed doors for yourself.

196.
Be creative with your resources and ask God to pour his inspiration in your little

ideas; as God multiplied the little loaves of bread and fishes. Jesus lifted them up, prayed, and fed the multitudes. You may want to find out how many baskets of remnants were collected afterwards.

197.
Although you must work hard, do all you can to delegate; it makes sense and prevents all the stress from lying in one zone.

198.
Once again, loosen the muscles on your face and laugh – just laugh.

199.
Take a retreat; pray, seek God's will and face – stretch out, rest in His presence; stop talking; listen, rest on Him some more – He may speak to you.

200.
Release yourself; pray - cry, groan, shout, plead, intercede, roll, cry some more; scream, shout, cry some more. Come out of your retreat, dry your tears, smile and face the task.

201.
Do not be intimidated into switching to small dreams; do not be intimidated into thinking that you are nothing, that you are going nowhere and that you cannot amount to anything.

202.
Take time off and play; try new and clean natural games. Jump in the sea or stream; swim, play – roll in the sand – get thrilled – become like a child once again. You need it – you certainly need that kind of break.

203.
Hit the ground and run with a smiling face. If you do not start, you will be on that same spot, crying, forever.

204.
Do not waste your time trying to explain your predicament or problem to everyone you see. They may not even be listening. If they do listen, they may not understand; and even if they do understand, they may not lift a finger to help; and if they do try to help, they may not be touching the real problem; and

some may be laughing and making fun of your situation. Let God direct you.

205.
Not all voices make sense. Some may be adding to your problems. Learn to discern.

206.
Be careful not to wash your dirty linen in public; it will not make it any cleaner. Ears want to listen to your story and eyes want to pry into your affairs; ready to blow things out of proportion.

If ye then, being evil, know how to give good gifts unto your children, how much more shall your Father which is in heaven give good things to them that ask him?

Matthew 7:11 - KJV

5.

JUST LAUGH - REJOICE

207.
Learn to practice staying in the peace and presence of God.

208.
Know that you always have your greatest insurance with God and a more blessed assurance in the word of God. No risks, fees, and no expiration date.

209.
Textbook examples may be relevant; but never leave out the prompting of the Holy Spirit. It's the best.

210.
Be prepared to make only clean deals. Do not be tempted to do contrary deals no matter how hard pressed you are financially.

211.
Restructure your timetable. Manage you time effectively and find out areas of slothfulness or laziness.

212.
Read and consult only books that have the solution to your needs. Too many ideas like cooks may spoil your plan.

213.
Flow towards and within the range of holy thoughts and actions.

214.
Put relevant structures in place; get organised in areas of your failings. You may need a course of study or learning.

215.
Do not allow a negative response to spring out of you as a result of other people's negative attitudes. This may block off your blessings and stop you from receiving from God.

216.
Think about joining a more positive network. Do all you can to be more

positive within a network. Contribute your ideas generously.

217.
Learn to ignore every negative comment from others; refuse to relate yourself to their words that put you down.

218.
God has created you to have dominion over your circumstances and situations. See the issue that you are going through as one that God has given you power over.

219.
Believe that according to the word of God, you will receive anything that you desire when you pray, and you will not be put to shame. Our problem often is that we faint while we wait and lose faith – thus not receiving what was almost in our grasp.

220.
Evaluate every aspect of your life. Be sincere with the results or facts you find

about yourself, and change things if you need to.

221.
Think about going to the ants to learn their ways; you may have to re-organise your working tactics. Aspire to be like the ants who work all through summer and rest in winter. You don't deserve an early grave.

222.
God may be trying your heart, and preparing you to learn to handle success, or He may be training you to learn to ignore or work with clues from criticism.

223.
Carefully re-invent your style, your mind set, your attitude, your goals, your perspectives, everything. Something great is about to happen to your advantage.

224.
Dial that phone – firstly to God in prayers. Tell him how you feel – pour out your mind to Him, leaving no stone unturned.

225.
Tell yourself that:
You will fight like a giant
You will tower above all stress
You will soar like an eagle
You will be lifted above all problems.

226.
Do not imagine that God has taken you out of his list of favourites. God still loves you and still thinks highly of you. So do not be tempted to fall back to sinful ways, or even backslide, thinking that you are no longer in God's list or a special member of God's family.

227.
You may be going through the darkest nights of your life, the dustiest and most crooked roads, and engulfed by the most depressing thoughts. You may think as though you are the only person in the world going through such woes at this time. Set your eyes on the victory of Jesus on that cross. He conquered darkness and you will too.

228.
Do not start thinking that all eyes are on you, and that everybody is talking about you. Other people have their own problems, and their thoughts about you may not be as negative as you think.

229.
Conduct a risk assessment. Look at all the areas of you business, your studies, and your life; and evaluate the areas that are prone to risks, or factors that may have caused your problems.

230.
Include more positive words in your speech, more positive ideas in your actions, and more positive words in your thoughts.

231.
Re-educate your mind. Look for useful resources to help you understand your problems.

232.
What have your network of friends done to advance your life? If they are negative, it is advisable that you

abandon them. If they are positive, make use of their ideas wisely. Be guided by God's promptings in all situations.

233.
Take your eyes off that spot where you fell; keep moving on. However, mind how you go, there may be similar pitfalls on the way, and they may be disguised. Do not think that you cannot slip and fall again.

234.
It is not impossible at this time for you to begin to lose your focus and faith on the power of God – especially when people offend you or challenge the living God in you. Remember that God humbled Pharaoh and Herod and still humbles great people who think that they can oppose God and go scot-free.

235.
See the armour of God as a protective shell that you can run into when the enemy is prowling around you. Don't leave home without it.

236.
Do not think that God will lunch you into instant success. God's ways are not our ways; and God may choose to do things gradually so that you would not rush and slip once again.

237.
Do not prepare a rescue programme for God. If you create a programme outside the mind of God, you may be coming back to the same problems, or walking in circles once again.

238.
Seek the mind of God as you plan to take decisions that will lift you out of your problem. Evolve a closer walk with God – see him as your great buddy at this time. Even if things do not go your way immediately, still hold onto God as you pray, confess and believe in His word.

239.
Seek first the kingdom of God; put God's programme first. Do not skip church services, prayer meetings and all activities that link you to God. The enemy

may have attacked you in order to shake your basic foundation with God and steal those aspects of your life that link you with God.

240.
You may have to go back to the secret place of the Lord that the Bible teaches about. Prepare to dwell under the shadow of the almighty God, drawing strength and spiritual life.

241.
Let the word of God be bountifully present in your mouth. Speak it out in great measure. This will stimulate your soul – your will, mind and emotions.

242.
God will take you through the thickest clouds; He will see you through the fiercest storm. Prepare to follow when He prompts you to leave your comfort zone, as He may be preparing you to be a carrier of His anointing. Spiritually deaden those aspects of your life that would render you unsuitable to serve faithfully.

243.
Break free from walls that the enemy has created around you; break free and flow into God's territory by faith.

244.
You may be down now – but project into the future. Imagine the time when God will deliver you and anticipate how you would celebrate your success.

245.
Make a covenant with God. Decide to keep your side of the covenant and God will never hesitate to play His part.

246.
Be forever grateful and thankful that Christ has come to give you life in abundance, whereas the devil comes to kill, steal and destroy.

247.
Work and walk with God to map out your next plan of action; see His word as your guide.

248.
Link your future and destiny firmly with God's word. Do what the word of God prompts you to and stay within the boundary of the word of God.

249.
Meditate on how God helped other individuals to get rid of their heaviness and pain.

250.
See yourself floating in the peace of God. Rejoice that you can stay in the presence of God; enjoy it, and plan to stay long in it.

251.
God wants you to be free; though you may have heard contrary words, God still wants you to be free.

252.
Many people put curses on themselves through the words they use to describe their situation. Do not be caught in that trap.

253.
Fear has no part to play in your progression. It will never advance you and will consistently limit you.

254.
God's thoughts towards you are marked with a positive future, purposeful life and hope. God's thoughts towards you are that of peace, not of evil; God wants to bring you to a better place.

255.
Ask God to give you dreams that would change your future forever; pray that you would be like one of the greatest inventors that God can use to affect your generation positively, and bring you to a new level of greatness and excellence.

256.
Do not abandon that vision that God gave to you. Your present situation is not a call to abandon the vision.

257.
The forces of evil may be prowling around, waiting for you to finally fail so

that they would destroy you. Do not quit the presence of God – the source of your protection.

258.
There should be no need for mediocrity; prepare to launch into the best and brightest level you can never imagine.

259.
Determine to dwell in obedience; there should be no compromise because God is holy.

260.
Once again, God would appreciate if you bless other folks as they hunger and thirst. This is the time for you to be generous even if nobody gives back to you.

261.
God knows how to take you out of this maze, and He will gradually put your steps on the right path.

262.
God is putting a new programme in place for you piece by piece, fitting it all together, like raw clay in His hands. Give him the opportunity to remould you into the vessel that is best for you.

263.
God's moulding process may be painful. It's not easy to give up old ways; but God will make the process of reconstruction bearable for you.

264.
Ask the Holy Spirit to deploy his Searchlight to probe and purge out every unwanted aspects of your life.

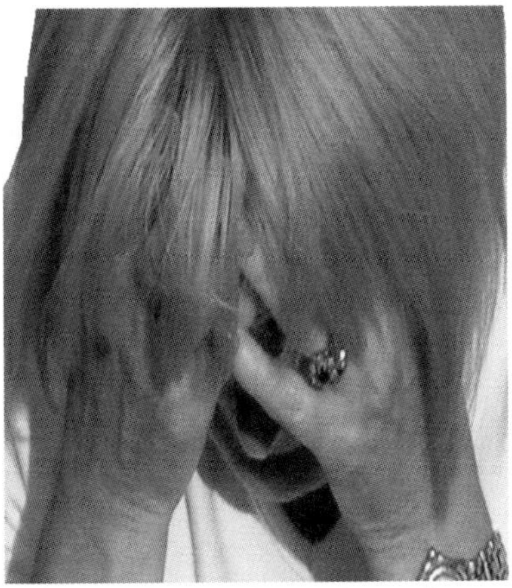

These things I have spoken unto you, that in me ye might have peace. In the world ye shall have tribulation: but be of good cheer; I have overcome the world.
John 16:33

6.
STAY ON THE POSITIVE SIDE

265.
Do not grumble; God is listening. It is the plan of the devil for you to crumble, falling flat on your face, and never to rise. Just give thanks and do not grumble.

266.
Be flexible, approachable and lovable in God's hands. Let all stiffness go as you relax in the hands of Jesus.

267.
The devil may be roaming to and fro the earth seeking for whom to devour, but God's eyes are roaming to and fro the earth, looking out to save and help you.

268.
Let your root in Christ be firm;
holding firmly to Christ the rock of life.

269.
Do not magnify the negative. See thorns as part of the plant that gives us beautiful blooming roses.

270.
Try, try, and try again.
Do not give up.

271.
Find positive people
Find positive places
Find positive ways.

272.
Don't entertain lies that are being whispered into your heart from any source. Dwell on the truth from God's word that you know and spin out the best creatively.

273.
Examine the words of men, testing every word with the word of God.

274.
Caution your feet and where they often take you to. You may be overstaying your welcome. Don't feel bad if you are

told that it is time to move on.
Be sensible; it's time to withdraw.

275.
Explore how your talents can open new doors for you. You were created with loads of gifts and talents – you may not have explored half of them yet.

276.
Be happy
You are here
Not in hell
Roasting or baking
Asking for a sip of water
Arguing with the devil
Shouting
Lamenting
Groaning
At least you are still here
Having hope in Christ
Enjoying the fellowship of believers
Not in company of deceivers
Be happy
You are here.

277.
It's time to turn your big guns of prayer at the enemy once again; pulling down his strongholds and breaking every yoke of fear and destruction.

278.
Tame it – anything - just tame it. Including any emotion that let you down; any excesses - tame them all, and claim your victory. You can do it.

279.
Clear any clutter – your excess possessions. Let the Holy Spirit help you to make choices with regards to all the junk that you have, thinking we are wealthy.

280.
Let go of the idea that everything can be solved in an instant. God will move in His own time, so do not stress yourself about anything.

281.
Explore alternative methods of getting your work done and ask God to help you to be more creative.

282.
Sort out your timekeeping. Ever heard of starting off early and 'early to bed and early to rise'?

283.
Do not be too uptight about anything – even disappointments. You never know, your disappointment may be a way of God having his way, or saving your life.

284.
Try to be more offensive in your prayers. Don't wait for the devil to attack before you begin to pray. Let your prayers rain down fire from heaven, taking control, and destroying the plans of the devil; victory is near.

285.
Do not fret about the way you are, but work on something – try to change something – even if it is just something simple like what you eat.

286.
You have to start doing things. If you do not start, you will never accomplish anything.

287.
Dump all junk mails that suggest and instigate compulsive shopping.

288.
Try to be more imaginative – think. Explore the world around you – see what could be of use to you in your situation. Think.

289.
Divine intervention may not be too far from the corner – pray.

290.
Learn to tap into the inner depth of God's power. Through being quiet and confident, you will find peace, joy and strength.

291.
Be determined to go wherever God sends you. Abraham believed God and was willing to go when God prompted him to move.

292.
Look around you; God is destroying the so-called wisdom of philosophers and

great thinkers and showing their knowledge as foolish. God is frustrating their plans and learning; and you may want to ask yourself if you really have to hold on to their vane ideas for too long.

293.
Let go, let God have His way in this situation you have found yourself.

294.
Speak positive words into every aspect of your life - your body, mind, spirit, projects, family, etc.
When last did you say something positive? Words that are never spoken can never be actualised or produce positive results.

295.
Let the best words flow from your mouth as you seek to motivate others.
Remember, what you give will be given back to you.
We reap what we sow.

296.
Do not try to please everybody for the sake of it and to your own detriment.

297.
Feel good about yourself
Feel good about your body
Feel good about your talents
Do not seek to be like others.

298.
Stay pretty calm
Stay calculated
Stay collected
Stay positively calm.

299.
Ask the Holy Spirit to teach you how you could negotiate yourself out of your negative situation.

300.
Do not worry.
It suffocates and stresses
It stagnates.
It dislocates and devastates
It destroys.

301.
You may sometimes see all forms of images, maps and ideas rushing through your mind. Ask God to lead you to the right calming and helpful choice.

Be still, and know that I [am] God: I will be exalted among the heathen, I will be exalted in the earth.
Psalms 46:10

7.
YOU CAN SAY 'IT'S FINISHED'

302.
Face any problem boldly; tackle it and win it, with God on your side.

303.
Create a new look; it could sell millions. Even absurd things make wealth. Think around your disappointment and explore an opportunity for creativity.

304.
It is about time to appreciate your source of strength – God.

305.
Think about David. He had an ordinary sling and stones, but that was not the source of his victory. What do you have to face the evil one? Let your faith rest in God and not what you have.

306.
When things go wrong still believe in what the old hymn says '…it is well with my soul'. Even if the enemy should throw all forms of dart against you, it is still well with your soul.

307.
Be satisfied
With a little tent
With a little crumb
With a little drop
Be satisfied
Things could be worse.

308.
Refuse to be intimidated.
Refuse to let the devil walk all over you.
Refuse to be made a scapegoat
Totally intimidated and bruised by all.

309.
Ask God for:
A new day
A new phase
A new page
Within and around you.

310.
Imagine how God created all the wonderful people, mountains, planets, and see how things work by His power. Trust God to respond to all unanswered prayers.

311.
You may be taunted by your enemies – but be assured that the enemy will not have the last word on your situation. Hold that closely to your heart.

312.
God can revive your spirit again. God can give you a new heart, a new mind and a new body.

313.
God has the ability to allow that stream of living water to burst out within you. Do not limit the flow – let it all out – let it flow.

314.
Do not revive old scars. Let old scars be old scars. If you dwell too long in the realm of old scars, they would turn into fresh wounds.

315.
Minister to your soul, giving good seed of God's word to it. What else can you eat that has such an everlasting value?

316.
Openly declare that God is good to you to all and sundry; proclaim it loud and clear on the highest mountain, the lowest valley and everywhere.

317.
Do not be tempted to see a fortune teller; God will reveal things to your heart and show you the future in simple dreams and revelations. Tune your heart to God, asking Him to reveal great things you have never seen or heard.

SOME RELEVANT BIBLE VERSES

YOU MAY BE WEAK; BUT HIS WORD SAYS...

Be strong and of a good courage; be not afraid, neither be thou dismayed: for the LORD thy God *is* with thee whithersoever thou goest.
Joshua 1:9

PROBLEMS ARE INEVITABLE

My brethren, count it all joy when ye fall into divers temptations; knowing this, that the trying of your faith worketh patience. But let patience have her perfect work, that ye may be perfect and entire, wanting nothing.
James 1:2-4

LISTEN

I will hear what God the LORD will speak: for he will speak peace unto his people, and to his saints: but let them not turn again to folly.
Psalms 85:8

YOU SHOULD HAVE KNOWN THIS EARLIER

And we know that all things work together for good to them that love God, to them who are the called according to his purpose.
Romans 8:28

FAITH EMPOWERS

And Moses said unto the people, Fear ye not, stand still, and see the salvation of the LORD, which he will shew to you to day: for the Egyptians whom ye have seen to day, ye shall see them again no more for ever.
Exodus 14:13

DON'T GIVE UP

We are troubled on every side, yet not distressed; we are perplexed, but not in despair; Persecuted, but not forsaken; cast down, but not destroyed.
2 Corinthians 4:8-9

YOU CAN OVERCOME

Therefore I take pleasure in infirmities, in reproaches, in necessities, in persecutions, in distresses for Christ's sake: for when I am weak, then am I strong.
2 Corinthians 12:10

REFUSE TO BE TROUBLED

Peace I leave with you, my peace I give unto you: not as the world giveth, give I unto you. Let not your heart be troubled, neither let it be afraid.
John 14:27

FEAR NOT

For God hath not given us the spirit of fear; but of power, and of love, and of a sound mind.
2 Timothy 1:7

PRESS ON

Remember ye not the former things, neither consider the things of old.
Behold, I will do a new thing; now it shall spring forth; shall ye not know it? I will even make a way in the wilderness, *and* rivers in the desert. The beast of the field shall honour me, the dragons and the owls: because I give waters in the wilderness, *and* rivers in the desert, to give drink to my people, my chosen. This people have I formed for myself; they shall shew forth my praise.
Isaiah 43:18-21

FREEDOM IS POSSIBLE

For ye have not received the spirit of bondage again to fear; but ye have received the Spirit of adoption, whereby we cry, Abba, Father.
Romans 8:15

FOCUS ON JESUS

Thou wilt keep [him] in perfect peace, whose mind is stayed on thee: because he trusteth in thee.
Isaiah 26:3

NO TURNING BACK

And Jesus said unto him, No man, having put his hand to the plough, and looking back, is fit for the kingdom of God.
Luke 9:62

PATIENCE COUNTS

With all lowliness and meekness, with longsuffering, forbearing one another in love...
Ephesians 4:2

SMILE

A merry heart doeth good like a medicine: but a broken spirit drieth the bones.
Proverbs 17:22

REFUSE TO BE OFFENDED

Great peace have they which love thy law: and nothing shall offend them.
Psalms 119:165.

FORGET THE PAST

Not as though I had already attained, either were already perfect: but I follow after, if that I may apprehend that for which also I am apprehended of Christ Jesus. Brethren, I count not myself to have apprehended: but this one thing I do, forgetting those things which are behind, and reaching forth unto those things which are before, I press toward the mark for the prize of the high calling of God in Christ Jesus.
Philippians 3:12-14

STEPS TO SALVATION & SPIRITUAL GROWTH

1. Jesus died on the cross of Calvary and shed his blood to save us. Only the blood of Jesus cleanses from all sins.

2. Confess your sins and repent; turning from all evil ways. Without repentance there can be no salvation. God is merciful to all who repent.

3. Ask Jesus to come into your heart, and accept Him as your Lord and saviour.

4. Read your Bible; meditate, think or ponder on the word of God.

5. Pray everyday, committing your ways and thoughts to God.

6. Attend a Bible believing church and contribute positively to the work of church growth and evangelism - telling others about the love of Jesus.

7. Ask God to fill you with the Holy Spirit. You need the power and ability to overcome the power of the flesh. The Holy Spirit is your helper, comforter, and guide. You cannot live a successful Christian life without His power.

8. Distance yourself from your past friends who lead you to familiar sins. Seek to tell them about Christ and do not be dragged back to the mud.

9. There is an active part that you have to play in your new life as a Christian. Discipline yourself and cut off all activities and conversations that would not please God.

10. Guide what comes into you heart at all times, and what goes out of your mouth.